Candles in the dark

a course to lead us into a deeper awareness of the ever-present God

David **Adam**

kevin
mayhew

First published in 2004 by
KEVIN MAYHEW LTD
Buxhall, Stowmarket, Suffolk, IP14 3BW
E-mail: info@kevinmayhewltd.com

9 8 7 6 5 4 3 2 1 0

ISBN 1 84417 285 6
Catalogue No. 1500718

Cover design by Angela Selfe
Edited by Marian Reid
Typesetting by Kevin Whomes

Printed and bound in Great Britain

Contents

DAVID ADAM was the Vicar of Lindisfarne, off the Northumbrian coast, for thirteen years until he retired in March 2003. His work involved ministering to thousands of pilgrims and other visitors. He is the author of many inspiring books on spirituality and prayer, and his Celtic writings have rekindled a keen interest in our Christian heritage.

Introduction

When the days are dark, or when the power fails, I love to light candles. There are times when life itself lacks power, when we struggle against darkness, then it is good to seek a light to disperse the gloom. Advent has the longest night of the year and the darkest days, perhaps that is why it is a special time of candle lighting. Think about the saying: 'It is better to light a small candle than to complain about the darkness.' Every day in Advent I light a candle to affirm that Christ, the Light of the World, comes to us, to you, to me. Advent is about the coming of light, the coming of the Lord to his people. I believe that our Lord has been coming to his universe since the beginning of creation. In fact, he has never left the world he has made. He comes now as he came in the days of old, and he will come until the end of time. Know that even now he comes to you. Make room for him in your home and in your heart. Be sure that you are not too preoccupied and therefore do not have any space in your days. Wherever you are, know that he comes.

When the days are dark and cold,
the Lord comes as he did to our ancestors of old.
When the way is unknown and our future uncertain,
the Lord comes as he did to our ancestors of old.
When we are in captivity and long to be free,
the Lord comes as he did to our ancestors of old.
When we are in the wilderness and hunger and thirst,
the Lord comes as he did to our ancestors of old.

When relationships are difficult and we need a loving presence,
the Lord comes as he did to the prophets of old.
When we fail in our faithfulness and need forgiveness,
the Lord comes as he did to the prophets of old.
When life is empty and chaos seems to have taken over,
the Lord comes as he did to the prophets of old.
When evil triumphs and we feel defeated,

the Lord comes as he did to the prophets of old.
When we are wrung out and are unable to rise,
the Lord comes as he did to the prophets of old.

When we struggle to be faithful and to say our prayers,
the Lord comes as he came to John the Baptist.
When we are willing to let go for the sake of God,
the Lord comes as he came to John the Baptist.
When we attempt to proclaim the gospel,
the Lord comes as he came to John the Baptist.
When we patiently await his coming,
the Lord comes as he came to John the Baptist.

When we wait upon the Holy Spirit,
the Lord comes as he came to the Blessed Virgin Mary.
When we trust in our God and commit ourselves to him,
the Lord comes as he came to the Blessed Virgin Mary.
When we say to God, 'Your will be done',
the Lord comes as he came to the Blessed Virgin Mary.
When we say 'Yes' to the call of God,
the Lord comes as he came to the Blessed Virgin Mary.

Every day can be a Christmas day,
for the Lord comes to us as he came to Bethlehem.
He seeks to be born in us,
for the Lord comes to us as he came to Bethlehem.
He wants us to come to him like the shepherds,
for the Lord comes to us as he came to Bethlehem.
He wants to live in and work through us,
for the Lord comes to us as he came to Bethlehem.
He comes eternally and seeks room in our lives,
for the Lord comes to us as he came to Bethlehem.

To those who are seekers and travelling in the darkness,
the Lord comes as he came to the wise men.
To those who are not sure of the way and get lost,
the Lord comes as he came to the wise men.
To those who keep looking and longing,

the Lord comes as he came to the wise men.
To those who are watching and waiting,
the Lord comes as he came to the wise men.

He comes to you today as he came yesterday.
He will come again tomorrow, as he came today.
He comes to you always.
Welcome him. Say, 'Come, Lord Jesus.'

Rest in his presence and be aware of his love.
Let his presence be a light to your darkness.
A candle in the dark.

Advent celebrates the coming of Christ in three ways: it celebrates the Christ who has come throughout history, but especially through the Virgin Mary; it celebrates the Christ who comes now and waits entrance into our lives and our hearts; and it celebrates the Christ who will come at the end of time. Though all are important, and it is necessary to understand all three ways, what we need most of all is to recognise the Christ in our midst and that our God comes to us. We need to be open to him who says, 'Listen! I am standing at the door, knocking; if you hear my voice and open the door, I will come in to you and eat with you, and you with me' (Revelation 3:20). Make Advent a time when you truly let your Lord into your heart and your home. Make sure your faith is at home in your home and you are at home with your faith. There are still too many Christians who speak as if God is something to do with church and churchgoing, when God is to be met in all his creation.

Each week in Advent, as the darkness increases, I like to light more candles. At the beginning of Advent it is good to prepare your Advent candles. Make this an act of worship in itself. Make an Advent wreath as an expression of your love for God and God's abiding love for you and all of his creation.

Making an Advent Wreath

You can get a circle of oasis from a florist and fill it with greenery, which reminds us we are dealing with eternal events. I like to use yew, holly and ivy, with a few holly berries to remind us of the sacrifice of Christ. Add to the circle four candles – I prefer to use purple candles for the season of Advent. In the centre of the circle put a larger candle of white or gold. This represents Christ and will be lit for the first time on Christmas Day, though it stands there as a reminder that he is always in our midst. A simpler wreath can be made by placing four candles on a small plate with the fifth candle in the centre. It is better to keep it simple than to not make one at all. This latter wreath could be created each week.

Six Weeks of the Christmas Season

The first week we will light one candle, in memory of the patriarchs, our ancestors in the faith. We will remember people like Abraham, Jacob, Joseph, Moses and David. We light this candle for the Lord who comes and seeks a living relationship with us. We also light it for adventurers in the faith.

The second week we will light two candles, one for the patriarchs, the second for the prophets. We will give thanks for Elijah, Elisha, Amos, Hosea, Isaiah, Jeremiah, Ezekiel, for the major and the minor prophets. We light this candle for the Lord who comes to guide us and bring us to his light. We also light it for men and women of vision throughout the ages.

The third week we will light three candles. The new candle is for John the Baptist and for us to think about how we make ready for the coming of our Lord. We light this candle for the Lord who will refresh and restore us. We also light it for all who have immersed themselves in the presence of God – Father, Son and Holy Spirit.

The fourth week the new candle is for the Blessed Virgin Mary, for the acceptance of God's will and the promise of the coming Christ. We light this candle for the Lord who seeks to work in us and through us. We also light it for all who have changed the world through their dedication and self-sacrifice.

At Christmas, all the candles are lit (perhaps as part of a service in church).

Week five should be as near Christmas as possible. We light all five candles. The world has received its Saviour, Christ is come to earth. We light the candles and give thanks that he has entered our world, that he has come down to raise us up. We light all the candles and rejoice that Christ is with us. We also light the candles to give thanks for all faithful pastors and ministers.

The sixth week we light the five candles and give thanks that Christ has come as the Light of the World, to destroy the darkness and to open the way to eternal life for us. We also light the candles for all who have sought or are seeking to know the presence of God and his love.

Actually, at home I like to light the candles until 2 February. This means the candles will have been lit for the forty days of the Christmas season, ending with Candlemas Day, the Festival of the Presentation of Christ in the Temple. I replace any candles that burn themselves out for God, though they can be left burned out as a memorial to those who have burned out their lives for God. Will we allow our lives to burn for his glory?

Making a Jesse Tree

The Jesse Tree is to remind us that Jesus had ancestors, as we do. There are two lists of the genealogy of Jesus in the Gospels: the St Luke list is in Chapter 3:23-37 and traces Jesus back to Adam, and the St Matthew list begins with Abraham in Matthew 1:1-17. When I read such a list in the Bible, it reminds me that every individual is important to God. Without these individuals history would not have been the same.

The easiest way to make a Jesse tree is to use a small Christmas Tree, or a large holly branch upon which we will hang different symbols each week. I have made a Jesse tree out of a bare branch which has smaller branches coming out of it. I have also made one from two large pieces of stiff board shaped like a fir tree and slotted together.

11

Each week we will add symbols to the tree which depict the story of our creation and salvation. You can start with the sun and moon, earth and stars to represent the beginning. You may like to add an apple as a symbol of the Fall; you can add Noah's Ark, a dove with an olive branch, angels on a ladder for Jacob, a burning bush for Moses, a harp for King David . . . be inventive and get people to make symbols and say why they made them. The Virgin can have a lily or a rose, or a cut-out picture of her from a Christmas card; in the same way you can add the shepherds and the wise men.

Let each week follow a definite theme; if the group is of any size it will be necessary to decide who will bring the symbols. I like to use the following pattern for symbols:

Week One
Adventurers in the faith, people like Abraham, Jacob and Moses. I like one or two examples of modern adventurers to be added by members of the group. Each time someone adds a symbol it is useful to say who it is and perhaps why they have chosen such a person.

Week Two
Discoverers in the faith, men and women of vision. Symbols of favourite visionaries or prophets. Again, it is good to add some present-day visionaries.

Week Three
People whose lives are immersed in the presence and power of God. Here will be John the Baptist and disciples of Jesus. Add our favourite saints and holy people of today.

Week Four
People who have risked all for God and doing his will. The Blessed Virgin Mary, holy martyrs, all who have sacrificed themselves for God. Again it is important to have examples from our own times. A crib and a cross could be added.

Week Five

Symbols of the shepherds and all who have cared for people and community. Remember faithful pastors and ministers.

Week Six

Symbols of the wise men, and their gifts. Remember other gifted people and all who have searched for God.

Each week I like to add one of the traditional symbols of Christ, to remind us that he comes to us. For this I would normally use painted eggs, though you can use table tennis balls. I have got children to decorate eggs each week which they will hang on the tree.

The symbols painted in bright colours are:

Week one: **IHS** – this is the beginning of Jesus in Greek. Though it is often said to be 'In His Service'.

Week two: the **Chi-Ro** sign – which is the first two letters of Christ in Greek.

Week three: **INRI** – which is the Latin inscription on the Cross, shortened, and which says: 'Jesus of Nazareth, King of the Jews'.

Week four: the **sign of the fish** – a drawing of a fish. In Greek the word for 'fish' is '**Ichthus**'. Each Greek letter stands for a word: **I** is for Jesus, **Ch** is for Christ, **Th** is for God, **U** is for Son, **S** is for Saviour. This was one of the earliest symbols of the Christian Church and it told of Jesus Christ, Son of God, Saviour.

Week five: the symbol of a **lamb** – for Jesus the Lamb of God who takes away the sin of the world.

Week six: The **star** – as a sign that 'Christ is the Morning Star', bringing in a new day.

This is a good opportunity to let children of the group share in creativity. One child, delighted to be painting an egg, said, 'Goody, Easter eggs for Christmas!' It is good for adults to be able to use talents other than words. The creating of the symbols can take the form of a time of quiet meditation at home. Sometimes, group members with families might like to make a tree for their home.

Obviously, if the Jesse tree is to be of use, partakers need to know what they are doing the week before, unless they will be able to work at it during the meeting, which is not usually practical. With the tree and the Advent wreath it is necessary for someone to get the basics ready before the first meeting.

If possible the Jesse tree should be brought to church on Christmas Eve. The Advent wreath could be brought also and the candle for Jesus lit during the service. The tree, the wreath and the crib could all be blessed as part of the Crib Service or First Communion of Christmas.

In each session I would like to use the same pattern, which I call the 'Five Finger Exercise'. For this to work it would be good if everyone had a copy of this book, as I think all members of the group should practise the exercise at home before they come to a meeting. We will not achieve much if we have not truly prepared ourselves for it, and we will get little out if we are not prepared to put something into it. This is often true of worship as well as study. Ideally, you will work at a passage every day of the week preceding the session: this way you will be enriched and be able to enrich the lives of others. The Five Finger Exercise, which I also call the 5p exercise, has a piece for each finger and all start with the letter P: Pause, Prepare, Picture, Ponder, Promise.

Pause

Pause in the presence. Stop whatever you are doing and be still. Make room in your life for God. Too often, we are so preoccupied that God cannot find room to enter. Clear a space each day, a space in your mind and heart as well as in your daily tasks. Begin by relaxing. Let go all tension. Let the body have rest. Check that your hands, your feet, your neck, are all relaxed. Let your breathing be natural and restful. Stop your mind from racing. Every time your mind wants to wander, bring it back with a word or two. You cannot empty your mind, it will want something in it. Say to it 'Peace' and let that peace fill your heart and mind. Peace in the presence. The deep peace of God: allow God's peace to fill your mind. Let that peace flow into you and about you. Say quietly, 'You, Lord, are here and with you I find peace.' Become aware of this reality and let it bear fruit in your life.

Prepare

We all need some direction, and so it is necessary to choose what prayers we want to use and which Bible passages we will read before we set out. This is like choosing a map or signposts to keep us in the direction we are hoping to go. To help, I have selected some prayers and a Bible passage for each week. The Bible passage for each week is printed out in full, though I do believe that it is good to discover your way around the Bible and know where various books are in relationship to each other. You may like to use a different version of the Bible to the passage that is written. The leader of the group should be familiar with the passages before the meeting, as should any who are to read them out loud.

Picture

After the passage has been read let everyone have a time of quiet to picture the scene. Imagining the event is very important for this is the only way it can truly touch us. Use all of your senses. What is going on? Can you feel the heat or the fear? What voices are to be heard, and who is reacting? Are there things you could touch or smell? If you were there, would you have liked to say anything? If you were making a film what would you need to include to make sense of this event – how would you like it to be seen and portrayed? Let the group try to build up a full picture of the event, including the emotions of the people involved. Building up such images is important to us for it helps us to become more sensitive and aware of the situation.

Ponder

Have a time of quiet when you think over the relevance of the events. These were ordinary people we have been talking about, though they have often been taking part in extraordinary events. Why are these people remembered? What message do they have for me? This is time to say where we stand on this matter and what direction we see from the event. What relevance does this story have for our lives and our community? Each person should be given the opportunity to say how he or she reacts to the story. Above all, we should try to listen to each other. So often God speaks through others to us. If we are not good at listening to others, it is not likely that we will be good at listening to him. We learn to give our attention to God by the way we give it to each other.

Promise

Promise that what we have learned we will put into practice. We may like to make a promise as a group, or we may decide to make a personal commitment to some action. We can end the session with a final hymn or piece of music and a prayer. Again, I will provide examples at the end of each session.

I assume that this book will be used for group meetings, though a person at home alone can easily use it too. Therefore I have assumed that there will be a leader who will help the group to prepare for and contribute to each session. If possible, it is good to have a different leader for each separate session. For the leader to be effective they must have worked at the session at home, preferably two or three times before the meeting. It might be best if they looked at it before each previous meeting, so that they can suggest any visual aids, newspaper cuttings, or photographs which the group might bring the following week. It could be useful for the leader to have a single piece of paper entitled 'Five Finger Exercise' with the guidelines for timing as below:

Pause
(10 to 12 minutes)

Have a time of candle lighting and quiet music, then some definite silence and stillness. If the leader is able to they could direct people into the relaxation by a few well-chosen sentences.

Prepare

(preparation should be no more than 10 minutes)

The leader should make sure that the necessary music, prayers and readings are at hand, as well as any illustrations. It may be necessary to check that there is plenty of room and seats, and also a CD player.

Prayer

Passage

Picture

(5 to 10 minutes)

Ponder

(no more than 15 minutes)

Promise

(5 to 10 minutes)

With the final prayers and music the whole session should be around an hour. It is important that the leader knows when to end each section and keep the whole session within an agreed time schedule. There is nothing worse than feeling trapped in meetings that last too long! If people decide to linger after a meeting, that is another matter.

As Advent is about the coming of a loved one, the Coming of God, we ought to capture the joy and excitement of that coming. Just as with any promised visitor, we have preparations to make – we may have to alter our daily schedule, even clean out a room. The important thing is to be as ready as possible for them and to enjoy being with them. For busy people this means pencilling space into your diary, making sure your day is not overloaded. It is no different in our dealing with God. For many it is not that they do not believe, it is that they do not give God space or time. Advent is a call to make room at your inn, to make space in your life, to be aware of the One who comes, and to enjoy knowing 'God is with us'.

SESSION I
Patriarchs and Adventurers

Leader to have made sure of music, reader of scripture, Advent wreath (or materials) and Jesse Tree (or materials) are all in place. It is often good for some quiet music to be playing. If it is possible, the group should understand about the Jesse Tree and be prepared to bring symbols of 'adventurers in the faith' and the IHS of Jesus.

Pause

Stop all activity and relax. Too many Christians justify their lives by action, by doing rather than being. Learn of the grace of God. God comes to you freely, undeservedly, and he comes now. Rest in the presence. You do not have to do anything. Make sure your body is relaxed, check it over. Are your hands and your legs relaxed? Is your head and neck relaxed? Get truly rested in the presence. If the mind wants to busy itself, stop it. Still the racing mind with a single word or idea. I often get my mind still by saying 'You, Lord, are here. You, Lord, are. You Lord. YOU.' I repeat this reality every time my mind wants to wander off and I use it to still myself in God's presence.

Prepare

You may like to begin in semi-darkness and after a short silence light one Advent candle for our ancestors, the patriarchs and matriarchs of old. Give thanks that God seeks a living relationship with us, with you. Add the characters to the Jesse Tree and, if possible, say why you have chosen that person (in a few words).

Prayer
The Lord is here.
His Spirit is with us.

Blessed are you, Lord God of our ancestors,
your light dispelled their darkness:

you revealed to them your presence and your love.
You spoke to them as you would to friends.
May we be aware of your coming,
rejoice in your presence,
walk in your light,
and abide in your love today and all our days.

Rejoice, for:
Goodness is stronger than evil;
love is stronger than hate;
light is stronger than darkness;
life is stronger than death;
victory is ours through him who loves us.

Desmond Tutu, *An African Prayer Book*
(Hodder and Stoughton, 1995)

Suggested hymns
• Hark, the glad sound
• Guide me, O thou great Redeemer
• Come, thou long-expected Jesus

Passage
Joshua 1:1-9

After the death of Moses the servant of the Lord, the
Lord spoke to Joshua son of Nun, Moses' assistant,
saying, 'My servant Moses is dead. Now proceed to
cross the Jordan, you and all this people, into the land
that I am giving to them, to the Israelites. Every place
that the sole of your foot will tread upon I have given
to you, as I promised to Moses. From the wilderness and
the Lebanon as far as the great river, the river Euphrates,
all the land of the Hittites, to the Great Sea in the west
shall be your territory. No one shall be able to stand
against you all the days of your life. As I was with Moses,
so I will be with you; I will not fail you or forsake you.
Be strong and courageous; for you shall put this people
in possession of the land that I swore to their ancestors

to give them. Only be strong and very courageous, being careful to act in accordance with all the law that my servant Moses commanded you; do not turn from it to the right hand or to the left, so that you may be successful wherever you go. This book of the law shall not depart out of your mouth; you shall meditate on it day and night, so that you may be careful to act in accordance with all that is written in it. For then you shall make your way prosperous and then you shall be successful. I hereby command you: Be strong and courageous; do not be frightened or dismayed, for the Lord your God is with you wherever you go.'

Picture

Joshua is on the edge of the Promised Land. See him standing on the bank of the River Jordan. This is his Rubicon; he must cross this as Moses crossed the Red Sea. He is aware of what lies ahead, the land is rich and fertile, but it is already occupied. There are walled cities, a great population, and it was rumoured that there were giants there. The people with Joshua were all for giving up and returning to Egypt. They had struggled this far, they were on the edge of a new life and they wanted to turn back. They were weary and now dejected. There had been promises, promises, promises. They had journeyed in hope and now it all seemed to have come to nothing. All that they had worked for seemed to have come to an end. It must have felt like their blackest moment and their whole future depended on it. Joshua spent time on the edge of the River Jordan, waiting upon God. Moses had commanded the people to 'Go forward' at the Red Sea. Now Moses was dead and Joshua was in command. No doubt he was aware of his own weakness and inner fears. What was asked of him was beyond human strength but he was not alone. God was with him and said: 'I will be with you as I was with Moses: I will not leave you or desert you . . . Be strong and stand firm. Be fearless then, be confident, for go where you will, Yahweh your God is with you.' Joshua was inspired by God, had his confidence renewed by God. He knew

21

that he was not alone. The God of Abraham, Isaac, Jacob and Moses came to him also. It was not in their own strength but in the strength of God they would go forward. Now he could face the people and lead them to the Promised Land.

Ponder

How often do we fail to step into a richer and larger world because of our fear, or because of the comments of the people around us? Too often we set out in our own strength and ability alone and we then run out of resources. In the words of a collect from the Book of Common Prayer, 'we have no power of our selves to help ourselves'. That we do not have the power does not mean we cannot achieve our goal. What happens to us is not just dependent on us. We have a power and a presence that goes with us. No matter what happens to us, what obstacles are put in our path our God come-to-us is with us, and we are on our way to glory.

The Patriarchs were men and women of faith. This was not about their belief but rather about their relationship with God. Faith was a living, vital relationship – not a set of credal statements. They travelled in his strength and power. Too often we are in danger of going alone into the unknown. It would be good to heed the words accredited to St Columba:

> Alone with none but thee, my God
> I journey on my way;
> what need I fear if thou art near,
> O King of night and day?
> More safe am I within thy hand,
> than if a host did round me stand.

When Abraham went out, not knowing where he was going, he went because he believed that God was with him. It was his relationship with God that gave him the power to move forward. He did not know where he was going but he did know who was with him. When Moses stood on the brink of the Red Sea it was his relationship

22

with God that enabled him to say to the people 'Go forward'. Moses was not depending on his own abilities but on the might and love of God, who came to him at the burning bush, and continued with him on his journey. Joshua discovered that God still comes and he comes now and to all his people.

When Joan of Arc was abandoned by her own people and given over to the English to be burned, she turned to those who betrayed her and said, 'It is better to be alone with God. His friendship will not fail me, neither his counsel, nor his love. In his strength I will dare, and dare and dare until I die.'

Realise that God calls adventurers, people who are willing to stretch themselves and to take risks. The safe and secure often find it hard to heed God's call. He calls us out of the shallows and into the deep. Many of the people God called were not particularly holy but they were willing to extend themselves and to reach out. If we never stretch ourselves or reach out, how can we hope to be in touch with the God who calls us from the beyond? Learn to adventure with God and in God.

Can we align ourselves with such people of faith? This will only be possible if we know our God, and it will only be possible if we are willing to spend time in his presence. The light that shines in the darkness is not of our own making; it is of God's power.

Look at the candle and know he is your light.
He comes to all who feel stuck in the wilderness.
He comes to the fearful, to whom the future is threatening.
He comes to those who are being overwhelmed, and to encourage wavering hearts.

He comes to all who feel alone, and to those who have lost their leader.
He comes to give courage, to fill us with new confidence.
He comes giving his presence and saying: 'I will be with you, my presence will give you rest.' He comes to you now, wherever you are.

His presence should make us more adventurous, for we do not travel alone. Our God is with us.

Promise

To practise the presence of God is to turn to him regularly during the day. Remind yourself of his coming to you, his presence and his love. Seek to stretch your abilities and your faith by adventuring with God.

Final hymn
- Make way, make way, for Christ the King
- Lord, the light of your love is shining (Shine, Jesus, shine)

Into our darkness, Maranatha.
Come, Lord Jesus.
Into our weakness, Maranatha.
Come, Lord Jesus.
Into our loneliness, Maranatha.
Come, Lord Jesus.
Into our fearfulness, Maranatha.
Come, Lord Jesus.
Come with your light.
Come in your power.
Come with your presence.
Come and encourage us, Maranatha.
Come, Lord Jesus.

> Let nothing disturb thee,
> nothing affright thee;
> all things are passing,
> God never changes.
> Patient endurance attains to all things;
> who God possesses in nothing is wanting,
> God alone suffices.
> And the blessing of God Almighty, the Father, the Son
> and the Holy Spirit,
> be upon us and our loved ones now and always.

St Teresa of Avila (1515-82)

Remind people to bring symbols for the Jesse Tree. Men and women of vision and all discoverers and the symbol of Christ.

Visionaries and Discoverers

Pause
Be still in the presence of God. Relax in his presence as you would in the sunshine. There is no need to do anything. Just enjoy being there with God. Make sure you are not too uptight or preoccupied: check that your body is relaxed and that your mind is at peace. Say quietly to God, 'Lord, you are here with me. Lord you are here. Lord you are. Lord!' Enjoy being surrounded and filled by God.

Prepare
You may like to start in semi-darkness and then light two candles. One for our ancestors in the faith and one for the prophets. Give thanks that the Lord is the light in the darkness of the world and that he comes to guide us. Add the symbol of Christ to the Jesse Tree and the symbols of visionaries and adventurers, saying briefly why they are chosen.

Prayer
The Lord is here.
His Spirit is with us.

Blessed are you, Lord God of all creation,
you created light out of darkness
and brought us to the glorious light of day.
Through men and women of vision,
you reveal your light and your presence to us:
you offer to us the glorious freedom of the children of God.
We come to walk in your light and in your love.
Blessed are you, Father, Son and Holy Spirit.

> May he give us all the courage we need to go the way
> he shepherds us,
> that when he calls we may go unfrightened.

If he bids us come to him across the waters, that un-
frightened we may go.
And if he bids us climb a hill, may we not notice it is a hill,
mindful only of the happiness of his company.
He made us for himself, that we should travel with him
and see him at the last in his unveiled beauty
in the abiding city where he is light and happiness
and endless home.   Bede Jarrett 1881-1934

Suggested hymns
• The Spirit lives to set us free (Walk in the light)
• Do not be afraid, for I have redeemed you
• We are marching in the light of God

Passage
Isaiah 43:1-7

But now thus says the Lord,
he who created you, O Jacob,
he who formed you, O Israel:
Do not fear, for I have redeemed you;
I have called you by name, you are mine.
When you pass through the waters, I will be with you;
and through the rivers, they shall not overwhelm you;
when you walk through fire you shall not be burned,
and the flame shall not consume you.
For I am the Lord your God, the Holy One of Israel,
    your Saviour.
I give Egypt as your ransom, Ethiopia and Seba in
    exchange for you.
Because you are precious in my sight,
and honoured, and I love you,
I give people in return for you, nations in exchange for
    your life.
Do not fear, for I am with you;
I will bring your offspring from the east,
and from the west I will gather you;

I will say to the north, 'Give them up,'
and to the south, 'Do not withhold;
bring my sons from far away and my daughters from the
    end of the earth –
everyone who is called by my name,
whom I created for my glory,
whom I formed and made.'

Picture

The prophet Isaiah, seeking to encourage his people and offering them strength for the new freedom that is being held out to them. Many of these people had been born into captivity and did not know what freedom was. They had dreamed of returning to their homeland, but in reality a good few would rather not make the perilous journey. They had food and security where they were and were now being asked to venture into the unknown. Were they strong enough to travel? Were they willing to sacrifice the present comfort for the desert and the difficulties that lay ahead? It was the prophet's task to offer them the strength of their God and his calling to his people. This was like the Exodus all over again. Freed from captivity they would be marching to the Promised Land. This was not a simple journey, there was the river Euphrates to cross and, beyond that, the desert. The prophet, like all prophets, declares to the people: 'God is with you; you are not going in your own strength but in the strength of God. As God was with the children of Israel at the waters of the Red Sea, he will be with you. As he was with Moses in the burning heat of the Negeb desert he will be with you. Do not be afraid, for the Lord is with you. God has chosen you.' As ever, God is calling and the people stalling. As humans they know they are not strong enough to make this journey alone: they know that for the moment they are safer where they are. But the prophet tells them of their noble calling, they are God's people and he calls them into freedom and to journey to the Promised Land. They are asked to see that they are not journeying alone. They are not going in their own strength, but in the power and presence of God. Do not fear, for God is near!

Ponder

God is with you today as you venture into the unknown, God is with you in your joys and in your sorrows. You are not alone in your journey. You are not forsaken in trial or tribulation, for God is ever with you. How often have you failed to venture because you felt alone and called to act in your strength alone? Know that you are not alone and that God is calling you to a more wonderful freedom and life than you have ever dreamed of. These words of Isaiah are still true:

> Do not fear, for I have redeemed you; I have called you by name, you are mine.
> When you pass through the waters, I will be with you; and through rivers, they shall not overwhelm you; when you walk through fire you shall not be burned, and the flame shall not consume you. For I am the Lord your God, the Holy One of Israel, your Saviour. Because you are precious in my sight, and honoured, and I love you . . . whom I created for my glory, whom I formed and made.

You are not only called by God, he knows you and your needs. He will bring his strength to your weakness, and dispel your fear with his presence.

Know that God wants us to seek newness in his world, to discover new insights and to learn new things. God speaks to us through the discoveries that are made, as they help us to extend our way of thinking and not live with a closed-circuit mind. We should seek to discover something new in each day and to give thanks to God for it.

Promise

Promise to spend a definite amount of time in God's presence each day, waiting upon him and speaking to him. Make sure that you do not face your fears and troubles alone: bring them to God. Promise to find newness in each day and make new discoveries.

Final hymn
- We'll walk the land with hearts on fire
- Colours of day (dawn into the mind)
- Lead us, heavenly Father, lead us

The Love of God go with you,
wherever he calls you.
May he guide you through the desert,
protect you through the storm.
May he give light in your darkness
and courage to your fearful heart;
and the blessing of God Almighty, the Father, the Son and the Holy
Spirit, remain with you always.

Remind the group to bring the symbols of Jesus of Nazareth, King
of the Jews, INRI and of people who are totally immersed in the work
of God. Make sure it is understood these are not all just 'church'
people.

John the Baptist and All Immersed in God

Pause

Make sure you are comfortable. Relax into the presence. Be aware that God wants to work in you and through you. Check that your hands and arms are relaxed, your feet are relaxed, and your face and neck are relaxed. It is amazing how many faces show tension. Let your mind be at rest. Picture yourself beside a lake or by the sea and it is all calm and bright. Enjoy being there. Know that God calls you into the stillness and brightness of his presence. If the mind wanders, bring it back by speaking to God. 'God help me to know that I dwell in you and you in me.'

Prepare

You may like to start in semi-darkness and then light three candles. One for our ancestors in the faith and one for the prophets, and one for John the Baptist. Pray that you are ready for the coming of our Lord to you. Give thanks that the Lord comes to refresh and restore us. Add the symbols INRI and of people immersed in the presence of God, saying briefly why they are chosen.

Prayer
The Lord is here.
His Spirit is with us

Blessed are you, Lord God of all creation,
to you be praise and glory for ever!
Your messenger, John the Baptist,
was a shining and burning light in the darkness.
He spoke the words of a prophet
and proclaimed forgiveness and the kingdom.
He prepared the way for the coming of the Lord.

May we share in his witness to the light
that true Light come into the world,
and rejoice that the Christ dispels our darkness.
Blessed are you, God, for ever.

Inspire us, O Lord, by the life and teaching of John the Baptist.
May we learn to live simply, that others may simply live:
let us turn to you each day and rise in your presence.
Let us seek forgiveness of all that is past and direction for the future,
that we may be heralds of Christ and prepare for his coming;
that we may live and work for his Kingdom, where you reign,
O Father, with the Son and the Holy Spirit; one God now and for ever.

Suggested hymns
• All over the world the Spirit is moving
• On Jordan's bank the Baptist cries
• Come, thou long-expected Jesus

Passage
Matthew 3:1-12

> In those days John the Baptist appeared in the wilderness of Judea, proclaiming, 'Repent, for the kingdom of heaven has come near.' This is the one of whom the prophet Isaiah spoke when he said,
> 'The voice of one crying out in the wilderness:
> "Prepare the way of the Lord, make his paths straight."'
> Now John wore clothing of camel's hair with a leather belt around his waist, and his food was locusts and wild honey. Then the people of Jerusalem and all Judea were going out to him, and all the region along the Jordan, and they were baptised by him in the river Jordan, confessing their sins.
> But when he saw many Pharisees and Sadducees coming for baptism, he said to them, 'You brood of vipers! Who warned you to flee from the wrath to come? Bear fruit worthy of repentance. Do not presume to say to yourselves, "We have Abraham as our ancestor";

for I tell you, God is able from these stones to raise up children to Abraham. Even now the axe is lying at the root of the trees; every tree therefore that does not bear good fruit is cut down and thrown into the fire.

'I baptise you with water for repentance, but one who is more powerful than I is coming after me; I am not worthy to carry his sandals. He will baptise you with the Holy Spirit and fire. His winnowing fork is in his hand, and he will clear his threshing floor and will gather his wheat into the granary; but the chaff he will burn with unquenchable fire.'

Picture

John the Baptist coming out of the Wilderness. He comes out of the Land of Desolation, out of the shimmering heat and emptiness like some ancient prophet. He must be mad to dwell there or else be a man of deep faith. No one could last in the desert without a strong faith. He is wearing the simplest of clothes made of camel hair, with a leather belt about his waist. For those who knew their Scriptures, Elijah was described as a 'hairy man with a leather belt around his waist' (2 Kings 1:8). Was this the great prophet come again as promised in the prophet Malachi (4:5)? For four hundred years prophecy had been silent and now John appears at the Jordan to 'prepare the way of the Lord'. Rumour has it he eats the locust or carob bean and wild honey, the simplest foods that the poor ate. The people will listen to him for he lives his own message. His simplicity of life challenges our complexities in living. His poverty of possessions points us to where true riches lie. They learned and believed that he was sent from God not to proclaim himself but to testify to the Coming One. He was not the Chosen One, but he was his prophet. Hear John say of Jesus, 'He must increase and I must decrease.' Will we allow the Coming One to increase in our lives? John proclaimed that before we can change the world we need a change of heart.

St John says of the Baptist: 'There was a man sent from God, whose name was John. He came as a witness to testify to the light, so that all might believe through him. He himself was not the light, but came to testify to the light' (John 1:6-8). John was come to proclaim a new day as the light was come into the world. Listen as he preaches and baptises in the Jordan. He calls all to be baptised and this gives him the nickname of 'the Baptist'. If this had taken place in the north of England, we would have called him 'Jacky the Dunker', for he 'dunked' people in the Jordan as some would dip a biscuit in their tea, until it is transformed. John asks people to allow their lives to be transformed and to live by the faith they say they believe in. See the people coming to be immersed in the waters, a symbol of washing, of being cleansed, a sign of renewal and a fresh start. This is to act out what they are called to do. They are to repent, to confess their sins and so to prepare for the coming of the Lord. Many are coming forward in penitence and faith, they are confessing their sins and seeking to lead a new life. They are seeking a change of direction and a change of heart and to be immersed in the saving power of God.

Ponder

Would you be found among these people, among those who know they are not worthy but that the Lord comes to them? Are you prepared for the reality that the Lord comes to you? Is your house and life swept clean and are you ready? Listen to John's word. He tells us to repent. You are called to turn around because you have been looking the wrong way and going in the wrong direction. Turn around and look to the One who comes. Do not wait for a far off time. I am always sorry for the rich young man of the Gospel – he had everything except real peace. The Gospel says he turned away from Jesus sorrowing 'because he had great riches'. It is too easy to let possessions or attitudes come between our God and us. He is here and comes to you. Turn to Christ. Think on these words from St Augustine:

O God, from whom to turn is to fall,
to whom to turn is to rise,
grant us in all our duties your help,

in all our perplexities your guidance,
in all our dangers your protection,
and in all our sorrows your peace.
Through Jesus Christ our Lord.

Learn to turn to Christ at the start of each day and throughout the day. Rejoice that he comes to you; the kingdom of heaven has come near to you. Say, 'Make me a clean heart, O God, and renew a right spirit within me.' You may like to think over and pray the prayer from *Hebridean Altars* (Moray Press, 1937) by Alistair Maclean:

I find thee throned in my heart,
my Lord Jesus.
It is enough.
I know that thou art throned in heaven.
My heart and heaven are one.

Like the people at the Jordan, confess and seek the forgiveness of your sins. Sometimes it is hard to even admit to ourselves we are not perfect. Have the courage to say 'I am not worthy, I do not deserve the love of God, I have in no way earned his coming.' It is then that you will discover the grace, the generosity and the forgiveness of God. As God forgives, you should learn to forgive yourself and others. To confess to yourself is the beginning, then learn to say sorry to those you have sinned against, and where possible to make restitution. Only then approach God, who comes to you, and say, 'Lord, I am not worthy to receive you but only say the word and I shall be healed.' In this way we are preparing the way of the Lord. Making room for him in our lives. Let us immerse ourselves each day in the power and presence of God.

I start this day
in the presence of the Father,
in the peace of Christ the Saviour,
in the power of the Holy Spirit.
I start this day
in the love of the Holy Three,
in the might of the Trinity.

Let John the Baptist, who came to bear witness to the light, lead us to the light of Christ.

Promise

To spend a time each day turning to Christ. To immerse, dunk, baptise ourselves in the presence of Father, Son and Holy Spirit.

Final hymn
• Dear Lord and Father of mankind
• Breathe on me, breath of God
• Take my life and let it be

God, the Creator, surround you with his presence,
Christ, the Redeemer, cover you with his love.
The Holy Spirit, the Strengthener, be about you to protect you.
That you may be immersed in the power and peace of God,
that the Holy Three may abide in you and you in them.
And the blessing of God Almighty, the Father, the Son and the Holy Spirit, be upon you and remain with you and your loved ones now and always.

Remind the group to bring the Fish symbol, Jesus Christ, Son of God, Saviour, and symbols of people who have changed the world by their dedication and their love for God. Bring symbols of Joseph and Mary.

The Blessed Virgin Mary and World Changers

Pause

Be still in the presence of God. Let all activity cease. Let go and let God. Let God have room in your life, let God have space and some of your time. You do not have to do anything at this moment. Relax. Let go of all tension, all agitation. Be still. Still the whirring of your mind and the movements and tensions of your body. Enjoy the quiet. If the mind will be determined to wander, bring it back to where you are. Breathe regularly and deeply saying with each breath you take in: 'Lord, you are here.' Then, as you breathe out, say, 'I come to do your will.' Let this be restful and joyful.

Prepare

You may like to start in semi-darkness and then light four candles. One for our ancestors in the faith and one for the prophets, one for John the Baptist and one for the Blessed Virgin Mary. We light this candle for the Lord who seeks to work in us and through us. Add the symbol of the fish to the Jesse Tree and tell of its meaning. Add Joseph and Mary and then those who have improved our world by their dedication and love.

Prayer
The Lord is here.
His Spirit is with us.

Blessed are you, Lord God of all creation.
To you be praise and glory for ever!
In the darkness of this passing age your light has shone out.
You have not forced yourself upon us,
but you only come if we so will it.
As we rejoice in the obedience of the blessed Virgin,
may we accept you into our lives and homes,

knowing that you have come to dwell among us.
Blessed be God for ever.

Lord Jesus, I give you my hands to do your work.
I give you my feet to go your way.
I give you my eyes to see as you see.
I give you my tongue to speak your words.
I give you my mind that you may think in me.
I give you my spirit that you may pray in me.
Above all, I give you my heart
that you may love in me your Father and all humankind.
I give you my whole self that you may grow in me,
so it is you, Lord Jesus, who live and work and pray in me.
I hand over to your care, Lord, my soul and body,
my prayers and my hopes, my health and my work,
my life and my death, my parents and my family, my
friends and my neighbours, my country and all people.
Today and always. Lancelot Andrewes (1555-1626), adapted

Almighty Lord God, your glory cannot be approached, your compassion knows no bounds, and your love for mankind is beyond human expression; in your mercy look on us and all your people: do not leave us to our sins, but deal with us according to your goodness. Guide us to the haven of your will and make us obedient to your commandments, that we may not feel ashamed when we come before your Messiah's dread judgement seat. For you, O God, are good and ever-loving, and we glorify you, Father, Son and Holy Spirit, now and for ever, to the ages of ages. Orthodox Liturgy

Suggested hymns
• Tell out my soul the greatness of the Lord
• Thy way, not mine, O Lord
• O come, O come Immanuel

Passage
Luke 1: 26-38.

In the sixth month the angel Gabriel was sent by God to a town in Galilee called Nazareth, to a virgin engaged to a man whose name was Joseph, of the house of David. The virgin's name was Mary. And he came to her and said, 'Greetings, favoured one! The Lord is with you.' But she was much perplexed by his words and pondered what sort of greeting this might be. The angel said to her, 'Do not be afraid, Mary, for you have found favour with God. And now, you will conceive in your womb and bear a son, and you will name him Jesus. He will be great, and will be called the Son of the Most High, and the Lord God will give to him the throne of his ancestor David. He will reign over the house of Jacob forever, and of his kingdom there will be no end.' Mary said to the angel, 'How can this be, since I am a virgin?' The angel said to to her, 'The Holy Spirit will come upon you, and the power of the Most High will overshadow you; therefore the child to be born will be holy; he will be called Son of God. And now, your relative Elizabeth in her old age has also conceived a son, and this is the sixth month for her who was said to be barren. For nothing is impossible with God.' Then Mary said, 'Here am I, the servant of the Lord; let it be with me according to your word.' Then the angel departed from her.

Picture

Many artists have tried to capture this scene. In some ways there is an amazing simplicity. This is an ordinary home; Mary is part of an ordinary family. No doubt she has to busy herself with jobs around the home. Yet, here it is another world, or the deeper reality of this world is seen. We could learn from this and discover God is at home in our homes. Dignity and meaningfulness comes with the territory – every place has the potential to reveal the holy – or it will be forever absent. Sanctity is part of our heritage. It comes with being human and is not earned but is to be enjoyed. We are great mysteries, as much as is the coming of Gabriel to Mary. The mystery of the presence is always with us to be enjoyed and not to be looked upon as a problem. In our ordinary surroundings God is as present as he is in any church. We all have our Annunciations, our own Nazareth, and our own Bethlehem, where the present is vibrant with the presence.

Here is a very young woman; only entering her teens, faced with a vision of the angel Gabriel – or more simply a message from God. The first part of the message is for us all: 'The Lord is with you.' Do you really take those words to heart? God is with you, he comes to you today as he did yesterday and will tomorrow. You are in his presence and in his love. You can ignore him if you want, but he will not leave you. Mary pondered over these words and you might like to do the same. Awareness of the presence often has a better chance of being revealed if we think over God's promises as Mary did. We know that though it was an ordinary home, it was here that Mary met with God. Picture the scene, see Mary doing ordinary tasks and then perhaps stopping to say a prayer, or to recite a piece of Scripture. She must have thought of Joseph and their forthcoming marriage.

Some talk as if visions were a delight: visions and a new awareness of God are always a little fearful – I prefer to use the word awesome – they are never commonplace. Mary has been chosen, not for her outward beauty, for her clever mind, or for her importance, though she might have all of these: she was chosen because she was ready to do God's will. Look at her: she is an ordinary young woman. She is engaged to Joseph the carpenter. Yet God chooses her because she is open to him and wants to do his will. For a moment heaven and earth, angels and humans wait to hear Mary's response. God wants her to be a special instrument, a special person. Mary looks a little fearful. 'Do not be afraid, Mary, for you have found favour with God.' Like Joshua, Mary is on the edge of a new world, a world that will change for us all due to her response. Mary is asked to be the God-bearer, to give birth to Jesus. Mary's response is 'How?' The reply is, through the power of God. In many ways it sounds like an ordinary conversation and yet it defies description. We must not lose sight of the fact that heaven and earth are one, they are not separate: at all times we are in God and God is in us.

God comes to his world, he comes to his own and his own do not receive him. Mary receives him by saying, 'Here am I, the servant of the Lord; let it be with me according to your word.' Mary's 'Yes' would change the course of the world. God would not force himself upon her, the choice was hers. She could accept him or reject him. Her acceptance of God's will is not simple. Joseph will have to be told, others will hardly understand. Doing God's will does not come cheaply but by doing his will the world is changed. 'Thy will be done on earth as it is in heaven.' The vision fades and Mary gets on with her daily tasks – but she knows God is with her and has called her to a special task.

Ponder

God is not restricted to churches and holy places; he is with us as we go about our daily work. There are not two worlds, heaven and earth are one. Julian of Norwich has said, 'We are more in heaven than of earth.' We miss this reality because we fail to stop and wonder at our existence. We ignore God, and the heaven about us, because we are so tied to things of the earth. We need to make moments in our days when we acknowledge 'The Lord is here. His Spirit is with us.' Learn to meditate on the wonder of your own being, the miracle of life, the mystery of creation and the presence of God in all.

Often the test is not do we believe, but rather are we willing to take time out to make our belief a reality and are we willing to obey? It is said the devil believes in God with fear and trembling – but he does not obey God. Do you really believe that God has created you and chosen you to pour his love upon you? He has called you to do his will and to take part in that service which is perfect freedom. Spend some time now rejoicing in his presence and accepting his love. Here are some words from *The Cloud of Unknowing*:

> Therefore strain every nerve in every possible way to know and experience yourself as you really are. It will not be long, I suspect, before you have a real know-ledge and experience of God as he really is. Not as he is

in himself, of course, for that is impossible to any save
God, and not as you will in heaven, both in body and
soul. But as much is now possible for a humble soul in
a mortal body to know and experience him.

The Cloud of Unknowing, trans. Clifton Wolters (Penguin Classics, 1970)

Promise

Promise to say throughout each day: Lord you are here. Your presence
is with me. Seek to be aware of your own Annunciations, your own
Bethlehem, Nazareth and Holy Land. Seek to know what God wants
you to do: this sounds easy but I know from experience it is not
easy.

Final hymn
• Be still, for the presence of the Lord
• Kum ba yah
• Jesus calls us here to meet him

May Christ the light of the world come to you
and fill your life with his glory.
May he give you the power to do his will
and serve him, whose service is perfect freedom.
And the Blessing of God Almighty, the Father, the Son and the Holy
Spirit, be with you and your loved ones always.

Remind the group to bring symbols of the Lamb of God, of carers
and adventurers. You may like to add a 'baby Jesus' to the Jesse Tree.

The Shepherds and All Pastors

Pause

Accept the greatest Christmas present of all – the presence of God. Come before Christ like the shepherds and adore him. Stop your busyness and relax in the presence. Make sure you are still in body and mind. Check over your body, your breathing for signs of tension and seek to relax them. Are your hands relaxed? Close your eyes and let them rest. Enjoy not doing anything but just being with God. If the mind wanders, bring it back. Each time your mind strays say: 'Come to my heart, Lord Jesus, there is room in my heart for you.' Above all, seek to make yourself aware that you are in the presence of God.

Prepare

You may like to start in semi-darkness and then light five candles. One for our ancestors in the faith, one for the prophets, one for John the Baptist, one for the Blessed Virgin Mary, and the larger candle for Christ come into the world. Let people add to the Jesse Tree, the baby Jesus, the symbol of the Lamb, and symbols of pastors and carers. Again, let each say why they have added these symbols to the tree.

Prayer
The Lord is here.
His Spirit is with us.

Blessed are you, Lord God of all creation,
you are our light and our salvation.
To you be all praise and glory for ever.
In the darkness of this passing age
you sent your Son to be our Saviour.
The word became flesh and now dwells among us.
He descended and became human

that we might ascend and share in the divine.
As we rejoice in your presence with us now,
let your love fill our hearts and our days
and your praises be on our lips.
Blessed be God for ever.

Lord, as we remember the shepherds in the hills above Bethlehem,
open our eyes to your glory,
open our ears to the songs of angels,
grant to us the joy of the shepherds,
that we may come to your presence,
bow before you in love and adoration,
and go on our way rejoicing.
Through him who shared in our humanity,
even Jesus Christ, our Lord.

Suggested hymns
• While shepherds watched their flocks by night
• See him lying on a bed of straw
• Come, come to the manger

Passage
Luke 2:8-20

> In that region there were shepherds living in the fields,
> keeping watch over their flock by night. Then an angel
> of the Lord stood before them, and the glory of the Lord
> shone around them, and they were terrified. But the
> angel said to them, 'Do not be afraid; for see – I am
> bringing you good news of great joy for all the people:
> to you is born this day in the city of David a Saviour,
> who is the Messiah, the Lord. This will be a sign for
> you: you will find the child wrapped in bands of cloth
> and lying in a manger.' And suddenly there was with
> the angel a multitude of the heavenly host, praising
> God and saying, 'Glory to God in the highest heaven,
> and on earth peace among those whom he favours!'
> When the angels had left them and gone into heaven,

the shepherds said one to another, 'Let us go now to Bethlehem and see this thing that has taken place, which the Lord has made known to us.' So they went with haste and found Mary and Joseph, and the child lying in the manger. When they saw this, they made known what had been told them about this child; and all who heard it were amazed at what the shepherds told them. But Mary treasured all these words and pondered them in her heart. The shepherds returned, glorifying and praising God for all they had heard and seen, as it had been told them.

Picture

The scene starts simply with shepherds looking after their flocks on the hills above Bethlehem. They lived out in the hills with their sheep, defending them against wild beasts or robbers. At least some of them had to stay awake and alert, watching for what happened in the night. No doubt they looked at the stars, they piled wood on to their fire, as shepherds did all over the world; there was nothing unusual about this scene. I often imagine this starry night. A shepherd throws a log on to the fire and the sparks rise upwards. He watches them ascend. Up and up into the heavens go the sparks. He watches as they fade from sight. Suddenly, without warning, it was as if the sparks were returning, as lights were coming down from heaven. The unseen world was appearing: the veil between them and the greater reality was being taken away. The angel of the Lord stood before them, and the glory of the Lord shone around them. Suddenly the hidden is revealed, another dimension is seen. In this ordinary place the glory of God breaks in, the world is vibrant with the presence and the mystery of God. What had seemed to be remote and far off was, in fact, part of their day-to-day existence. God was concerned about them and with them. The shepherds and glory became one.

Their reaction was one of fear; they hid their faces and were troubled. But the voice rang in their ears, 'Do not be afraid.' This is one of the commonest sentences in the scriptures. I am told this

45

sentence appears 365 times in the scriptures. Perhaps this is to remind us that every day we should dispel our fears and come before the glory of God. We have heard the words 'do not fear' said to Joshua and to Mary. God comes to us in love and in peace; God comes to care for us and to protect us. This is not a destroying or vengeful power. This is a God of love who cares for his creation and comes to it to bring it his presence and his peace. So the angel speaks to the shepherds, 'Do not be afraid; hear the Good News. To you, yes, to you shepherds, and to all people, here is news of great joy: to you is born this day in the city of David a Saviour, who is the Messiah, the Lord.'

To these ordinary working men on the hillside came a glimpse of the glory of God. They were not separate from God or in another world separate from God; their world and God were one. The sign of God's presence and message could not be more simple: 'You will find a child wrapped in bands of cloth and lying in a manger.' The great moment of God's coming revealed in the birth of a child in a cave used to house cattle. God is to be found amid the straw and the cows. God is not far off or relegated to events of the past: he comes now and is found among us.

Once again glory breaks in, the multitude of the heavenly host are heard saying, 'Glory to God in the highest heaven, and on earth peace among those whom he favours'. God and earth, angels and humans are mingled together and it is always so, if we are alert enough and our hearts are tuned to it.

Suddenly the scene becomes quite normal again. The shepherds are on the hillside and the angels are neither seen nor heard. Was it a dream? Was there any reality to their glimpse of glory, to their vision in the night? As always visions must be tested. 'Let us go now to Bethlehem and see this thing that has taken place, which the Lord has made known to us.' So they went with haste and found Mary and Joseph, and the child lying in the manger. What they saw was terribly ordinary, if anything on earth is ever ordinary, a little newborn baby and its mother. Is not every birth a miracle? There were no haloes, there was the smell of cows, no heavenly songs, only the cry of the baby. But they knew there was more to it; they knew something far deeper than was visible. They were delighted to see the child. When they left for the hills, they 'returned, glorifying and praising God for all they had heard and seen'. Some would say that the shepherds were the first evangelists, for they were the first to see the Christ and go out glorifying and praising God.

Ponder

How have we allowed the world and our lives, which are so full of glory and mystery, to have become so commonplace, and even dull? We should take to heart the words of the poet Francis Thompson:

The angels keep their ancient places;
turn but a stone, and start a wing!
'Tis ye, 'tis your estranged faces,
that miss the many-splendoured thing.

Most things, if not all, are full of mystery if we look long enough and deep enough. We are so keen to move on that we often miss the glory that is presented to us. The shepherds had to be alert and to keep their senses keen. We often allow our senses to become dull and think it is the world around us that is dull. To those who have a living relationship with God, the world is always revealing wonder upon wonder. We need to take time to tune our hearts to the beauty and the mystery that is all around us. One of the ways of doing this is to meditate on the presence of God, spending a few minutes at least every day basking in his glory.

Sadly, many Christians talk as if heaven was far away. Some will even sing, 'There is a happy land far, far away.' Heaven is not far off. Remember Jesus proclaimed, 'The kingdom of heaven is at hand.' Heaven is close to each of us, seeks to be part of our lives now. Do not put it off until some future time: seek to discover the glory and presence that is ever with you.

Promise

Promise to rejoice that God is revealed in and through his creation. Say throughout each day, 'The Lord is here. His Spirit is with us', or say, ' God unseen yet ever near, thy presence may we feel.'

Final hymn
- Child in the manger
- Infant holy, infant lowly
- The Virgin Mary had a baby boy

The good and gracious God
grant you a glimpse of his glory.
May his angels defend you,
his presence go with you,
his light guide you,
his love surround you.
And the blessing of God Almighty, the Father, the Son and the Holy
Spirit, be upon you and your loved ones now and always.

Remind members of the group to bring symbols of 'Christ, the
Morning Star' and of seekers. They could also bring the three wise
men as individuals and also their gifts.

SESSION 6
The Wise Men and All Seekers

Pause
Know that there is no need to seek God, for he is here with you. Relax in his presence and rejoice in his love. Stop all your activity and give yourself, your time, and your talents to God. Seek to be still and rest in God. We are all seekers, but we also need to know when we have arrived and enjoy being there and being with him. Check for any signs of tension in your body and in your life, seek to bring the peace of God to them. If the mind wants to wander, use a few words to keep it in check. You may like to say: 'You, Lord, are here. You, Lord, are. You, Lord. You'. This is an affirmation of the reality of the presence. Rest in its truth.

Prepare
You may like to start in semi-darkness and then light the five candles, rejoicing that Jesus is the Light of the World. Add to the Jesse Tree the star, the wise men and their gifts and symbols of seekers. Let each say why they have placed their symbol on the tree.

Prayer
The Lord is here.
His Spirit is with us.

Blessed are you, Lord God of all creation,
from the rising of the sun to its setting,
your glory is proclaimed in all the world.
Your presence has brought light to our darkness
and a new radiance to the world.
As you call us into his marvellous light,
may we offer our lives and talents to you,
may our lips proclaim your praise,
and may we go on our way rejoicing.
Blessed be God for ever.

O God lighten our journey and direct our way.
As we seek your presence and long for you,
lead us until we come before the Child of Mary:
guide us until we bow in love and adoration.
As we remember the journeying of the wise men,
and the offering of their gifts,
help us to give our hearts to Christ,
and to spend our lives in his service.

Suggested hymns
• As with gladness men of old
• O worship the Lord in the beauty of holiness
• Wise men seeking Jesus travelled from afar

Passage
Matthew 2:1-12

> In the time of King Herod, after Jesus was born in
> Bethlehem of Judea, wise men from the East came to
> Jerusalem, asking, 'Where is the child who has been
> born king of the Jews? For we observed his star at its
> rising, and have come to pay him homage.' When King
> Herod heard this, he was frightened, and all Jerusalem
> with him; and calling together all the chief priests and
> scribes of the people, he inquired of them where the
> Messiah was to be born. They told him, 'In Bethlehem
> of Judea; for so it has been written by the prophet: "And
> you, Bethlehem, in the land of Judea, are by no means
> least among the rulers of Judah; for from you shall
> come a ruler who is to shepherd my people Israel"'.
> Then Herod secretly called for the wise men and learned
> from them the exact time when the star had appeared.
> Then he sent them to Bethlehem, saying, 'Go and search
> diligently for the child; and when you have found him,
> bring me word so that I may also go and pay him homage.'
> When they had heard the king, they set out; and there,

ahead of them, went the star that they had seen at its rising, until it stopped over the place where the child was. When they saw that the star had stopped, they were overwhelmed with joy. On entering the house, they saw the child with Mary his mother; and they knelt down and paid him homage. Then, opening their treasure chests, they offered him gifts of gold, frankincense and myrrh. And having been warned in a dream not to return to Herod, they left for their own country by another road.

Picture

There are many things we do not know about the wise men. They appear so briefly and then disappear again. We do not know that there were three: we assume this by their gifts. We do not know for a fact that they were kings, though at least they must have been men of some standing to gain an entrance to the court of Herod. We do know that they were seekers and travelled by night, for they followed a star. We also know that they came out of the lands in the east, possibly Persia and Mesopotamia. They were wise men steeped in learning. They were rich men and perhaps travelled with a retinue of protectors. Try and picture them travelling by night and attempting to sleep during the day. Most people that they met must have thought them a little odd. No doubt friends and relatives tried persuading them not to go on such a hazardous journey. Travelling in strange lands to an unknown destination was bad enough, but they would be at risk from robbers and wild beasts. Why leave their comfort and security? What was it that was calling them out from where they were? These were questions hard to answer, but we all know there is more to life than security. They all wanted to see Jesus, the mind cannot explain this, but the heart can understand it. They would risk all they had, even life itself, to come before the Christ child. Legend says there was another wise one who did not come to Jesus and he is left wandering for ever – can that be you? These seekers knew what Augustine meant when he said, 'Our hearts are restless until they rest in you.'

Picture the wise men as they travel by night. The air is cold, the way is dark. Their eyes are fixed on a star, they are journeying westwards. The pace is quite slow as darkness hinders their way. They will travel until the star fades from the sky and the dawn comes. Then they will pitch tent and seek to rest. They have to travel as lightly as possible to make the journey as easy as possible. It must have been hard to sleep in the heat of the day. These men are taking risks and making sacrifices. Were they ever footsore or saddle sore and weary? What was it that drove them on? They would not give up and they would not turn back. More than following a star, they were seeking to bring reality to their vision.

Their gifts are almost as mysterious as the wise men themselves, yet we do know that all these gifts were precious in the ancient world. Perhaps each gift made its own statement. Gold has always been a sign of power, and the symbol of a king. Could this gift have come from a king coming to bow before a king? Certainly it was the offering of what the world counted as most precious. Some people's pockets are as hard to touch as their hearts. This was indeed an offering of worth. More important was that the wise man offered himself.

Frankincense was used in worship, burnt away in adoration, used by priests; was this from a priest coming to worship a priest? Why did he have to travel all this way, could he not have offered worship to God at home? Incense is an offering before the mystery of God and the more we learn, the more we know there is to learn. For some, worship is offered regularly but they seem to stand apart from it. They offer sacrifices and gifts but do not offer themselves. Here the important offering is the bowing of the wise man before the Christ child. Incense was the symbol of his offering of himself.

Myrrh was used by sufferers to relieve pain and also used in embalming. Was this brought by one who suffered much to one who was destined to suffer and to die to relieve our distress and disease? Perhaps the journey was a painful one for this man, or maybe he had lost a loved one, or again, he may have realised that his own time was short. It is a strange gift to bring before a child but it does not ignore that life is not all sweetness. Once again, what mattered was that this man of sorrows came and offered himself to the Christ child. We can speculate about the gifts, but the important act for the wise men is that they came and offered themselves. They came to see him and worship him.

Ponder

What some dream about, talk about, others seek until they find. This is what our world needs, what we need: people who will have left the theory for reality, who leave the book behind and come face to face with the living God. We need people who do not talk of God as history, but as the living Lord. We want them to say to us: 'I have seen the Lord. As we sought him he 'came to us and made his home with us'.

John the Baptist said, 'Look, here is the Lamb of God' (John 1:36)

Jesus invited Andrew and another disciple, 'Come and see' (John 1:39)

Andrew said to Simon, 'We have found the Messiah . . . he brought Simon to Jesus' (John 1:41-42)

Philip said to Nathanael, 'Come and see' (John 1:46)

After the resurrection one after another will say 'I have seen the Lord.'

Mary (John 20:18)

Cleopas and companion at Emmaus (Luke 24:31)

Disciples (John 20:25)

Thomas (John 20:27)

Each came to see the living Lord. The invitation is to you, Come and see.

> So shut your Bible up and tell me
> how the Christ you talk about is
> living NOW. Sidney Carter

As with gladness men of old
did the guiding star behold,
as with joy they hailed its light,
leading onward, beaming bright;
so, most gracious Lord, may we
evermore be led to thee.

William Chatterton Dix (1837-98)

What can I give him, poor as I am?
If I were a shepherd, I would bring a lamb,
if I were a wise man, I would do my part,
yet what can I give him – give my heart.

Christina Rossetti (1830-94)

We need to seek until we find. We need to let reality test our vision. We also need to know when we have arrived so that we can come before him and offer ourselves. God wants us more than any gift from us. He wants a living, vital relationship with us, a sharing of love.

Promise

Promise each day to seek his presence and to bow before your God. Offer him your talents, your love, yourself.

I bow before the Father, who loves me.
I bow before the Son, who saves me.
I bow before the Spirit, who guides me.
I bow in love and adoration,
this day and for ever.

Final hymn
* We three kings of orient are
* What child is this who, laid to rest
* In the bleak mid-winter

God who, by the leading of a star,
brought the wise men to the Christ child,
guide your journey and your seeking,
until you get a glimpse of his glory,
and rejoice in his presence.
And the blessing of God Almighty,
the Father, the Son and the Holy Spirit,
be upon you and all your loved ones
this day and for ever.

The group may like to use this act of praise at the end of each
session, or when the whole course is finished:

Rejoice, for Christ comes: **he is a light in our darkness.**
He comes as of old, to those on the edge of a new day,
to those fearful and wanting to turn back,
to those with hard decisions to make,
to those who have been long in the desert. He comes.
Rejoice, for Christ comes: **he is a light in our darkness.**

He comes to all who are being challenged,
to those who are being overwhelmed,
to those who are facing a fiery ordeal,
to those longing for freedom,
to all who are seeking a better world. He comes.
Rejoice, for Christ comes: **he is a light in our darkness.**

He comes to those who live in simplicity,
to those who thirst for justice,
to those who hunger for righteousness,
to those who repent of their sins,
to those who turn away from evil. He comes.
Rejoice, for Christ comes: **he is a light in our darkness.**

He comes to those who seek to do his will,
who wait upon his word;
to all who magnify his name,

to all who rejoice in him as Saviour,
to each of us in our homes. He comes.
Rejoice, for Christ comes: **he is a light in our darkness.**

He comes to ordinary working people,
to all who are awake and alert,
to those going about their daily work,
to those who care for his creation,
to the humble and the meek. He comes.
Rejoice, for Christ comes: **he is a light in our darkness.**

He comes to the seekers and the searchers,
to all who will not be put off,
to those who travel in darkness,
to those not sure of their journey,
to everyone who offers their heart to him. He comes.
Rejoice, for Christ comes: **he is a light in our darkness.**